CONTENT MARKETING

50

Ways to Tell Your Story

(Insider Secrets to Better Branding)

SHERRY BECK PAPROCKI

R.S. Rock Media, Inc.
Granville, Ohio
2015

Library of Congress Cataloging-in-Publication Data

Paprocki, Sherry Beck

  [Content Marketing: 50 Ways to Tell Your Story]

(electronic/multiple format) -- ISBN 978-0-9963065-0-8
(electronic/epub)

  1. Nonfiction—Business Marketing 2. Content Marketing.
  3. Writing. I. Paprocki, Sherry Beck.

TABLE OF CONTENTS

SECTION I

Good writing can do wonders for your brand's story. Learn the secrets that experts know will make your story stand out among the clutter.

SECTION II

Does your website replicate well on mobile devices? Have you incorporated a blog? Learn insider tips about creating a website that gets your guests to linger.

SECTION III

Social media strategists know that good storytelling doesn't take a lot of words. Learn which social site best caters to wealthy teens, which is best for building any business and more tips for telling your unique brand stories.

SECTION IV

Your brand's story grows only stronger when you dig deep for research that provides a hearty foundation. Read what expert writers know when it comes to weaving intricate facts into fascinating stories that make waves in your industry and create good vibes for your brand.

Digital tools such as Vine and YouTube are only the beginning when it comes to putting your brand's image out in the world. Learn what publishers and producers know about getting the best visuals possible and other details of today's digital and print publishing worlds.

Publishing and broadcast companies have spent millions to keep ahead of the curve when it comes to modern communications. Insiders know that connecting with media personalities on social media and more can put the spotlight on your brand's story.

Every business and nonprofit is its own publisher in today's world. With opportunities to create e-books, custom magazines, blogs and more, an editorial calendar—and all of its components—will help you communicate a consistent brand message.

Stage an event, give a workshop or plan myriad other opportunities to talk about your brand's story. By powering up your marketing strategy, you'll learn how to use social media and other tools to make ripple effects around your brand's central story.

INTRODUCTION

A vast array of digital tools has rocked our world. This digital disruption, involving social media and more, provides you with new opportunities to help your brand stand out from the crowd. Here is a checklist of the 50 best ways to tell your story and tips about finding the people who can help you do that in the most cost-effective manner possible.

This is a list for the convenience of small business owners who know the importance of telling their stories but have limited time to do so. The Content Marketing Institute cited statistics saying that the best marketers use an average of 14 different marketing tactics and seven social media platforms in today's modern world.

Who has time to accomplish all of this on your own?

Yet, if you are well equipped to tell your story that gives you an opportunity to become the most disruptive brand among your competitors, drawing more attention from potential customers and clients.

I'll use an example from a client I work with, an attorney, who has been working hard to promote his brand for the last six, or so, years. In addition to his law practice that focuses on land use rights, he also has a land title company and a gas and oil consultancy. He has accomplished a significant amount of civic work in which he's donated his time to preserve open green space. This attorney also now invests in the businesses of young entrepreneurs.

As you can see, he does a lot of different things, even though they're closely related. The attorney realized that his brand was splintered and his websites needed refreshed. He's partnered with me to do that, create social media profiles, write articles for his e-newsletters and more.

About four years ago he decided to create a very upscale brochure on heavy, recycled paper that told his story and included good photographs of some of his development projects. The designer I often pull into these projects did a terrific job, as did the printer. Immediately upon receiving it, some of this attorney's top clients—big developers in the city where he lives—called him to say they were very impressed.

This may sound like an expensive endeavor. In fact, it is not. On average, this attorney pays less than $8,000 per year for his marketing efforts. In return, he gets a full team that I pull together—a designer, a web guru, a photographer and others—depending on his needs.

His return on investment has been much more than he has invested. In the year after he sent the brochure, his title business grew exponentially. His legal work involving land rights continues to grow as we promote the court cases that he has won. Being an environmental preservationist, potential clients can easily find him online because we've woven his civic work into his business brand.

Whether you're known as the blogging dentist, the Facebooking boutique owner or the Tweeting chef, you have the ability to fast become a brand that stands out. That type of activity will help you create ripple effects, gain more media coverage, speaking opportunities and other recognition that leads to a bigger bottom line for your business.

With so many opportunities to communicate with your customers and clients, it's important to tell your brand's story in a vibrant and unified manner across all platforms that apply. I promise that *Content Marketing: 50 Ways to Tell Your Story* will help your message rise above the clutter.

Start with a website audit. Are you communicating the story that is most important for your business? Business owners are usually too close to see the power of their personal story and how it propels their business forward, as it has done for my attorney client.

That's why I suggest hiring an independent writer to help you. A professional writer who is skilled at the art of storytelling can help you create a consistent, lively and engaging brand message for your business.

Digital storytelling is important and there are other opportunities to be in front of your potential customers and clients, too. Today, you need to embrace the idea of blogging about your industry, use social media, create white papers, write e-books, organize slide shows and access other techniques.

In 2009 when I was the co-author of *The Complete Idiot's Guide to Branding Yourself* (Alpha) few thought that social media would become the creative marketing tool that it has grown into. My editor at Penguin had to convince her editorial committee that such a book was necessary, in fact.

Today, the term *personal branding* is common. Facebook, Instagram, Twitter, LinkedIn, YouTube and more can deliver small snippets of information to your target audience. Not only can you communicate your brand this way, you can also easily get the analytics available to see if you're being successful.

But it's not all about digital. Even with rising paper costs and a greater environmental consciousness, there are still times that you may want professional products printed on good—hopefully recycled—papers.

Why are we still talking about print? Print provides an opportunity for a highly impactful vehicle that attracts attention. As new content marketing options have emerged, those willing to spend money on high quality print products have a greater opportunity to market a brand in precious ways. Be sure, though, the era of printing blurry products on flimsy papers is past. Do it well, or don't bother with print.

My company—R.S. Rock Media, Inc.—produces digital products and custom magazines for publishing companies, small businesses, nonprofits and other organizations. I've noticed a growing desire among those groups to create upscale, well-designed publications that are distinctly targeting their audiences with interesting storytelling. We have produced such magazines for real estate agents, hotels, yacht clubs, wine festivals and others.

Why Hire a Professional Writer?

It doesn't matter how long you've been in business, if you don't have a fully staffed marketing and communications department, this guide may seem overwhelming.

So, hire the best writer you know and get started. Any non-fiction writer who is a skilled interviewer, knows how to do detailed research and tells good stories will be help you accomplish any—and all—of the following tasks.

Google organizations such as the American Society of Journalists and Authors, the Society of Professional Journalists and other professional writing groups to find an independent writer in or near your community who brings the kinds of skills necessary to help you communicate well in today's marketplace.

This book is divided into eight sections:

1. Write Your Story

2. Refresh Your Website

3. Upgrade Your Social Media

4. Mine for Golden Opportunities

5. Get Visuals and Sound

6. Connect with Community Media

7. Engage with an Editorial Calendar

8. Power Up Your Marketing Plan

Section I
Write Your Story

Your brand's story is the heart of your business and, with good storytelling, it can be used to create a lasting bond with your customers. Even though I've been an independent journalist and author for more than 20 years who has written about high-profile personal brands such as Ellen DeGeneres, Katie Couric and Oprah Winfrey, I also write a lot of branding stories for private clients. *Everyone* has a very personal story about why they're in business. Sometimes it just takes an expert interviewer to peel back the layers to reveal that story.

Within the last few years, I've interviewed and written about a jewelry designer who was knighted in Hungary and eventually opened a shop in Austin and a real estate agent who reared her children on an isolated island and then used her experience to sell high-end homes there. Both of these people have very interesting stories about their business brands.

By telling their personal histories, they are successful at differentiating themselves from others in their businesses. That helps them stand out from the crowd of other jewelers and real estate agents with whom they compete. Their return on investment is increased interest from potential customers and clients who want to meet with them—and buy from them.

This is why I suggest you hire an expert writer for your story. As a business owner, you have many responsibilities. And, even though you or someone on your staff may be a good writer, there is no replacement for hiring a skilled professional who is practiced in the art of writing interesting stories.

To start, your branding story should be an authentic, relevant and transparent depiction of your business. This is the first of 50 ways that you can leave behind your competition.

1. A Branding Story

Once your branding story is complete, you can use it on your website's home page to introduce your customers and clients to your services.

A branding story describes your business and the unique skills that you bring to your customers and clients. It should be three to five paragraphs, or about 500-700 words. Creating this story is one of the most important projects you'll do because it is the basis for many other communications.

During the process of writing this story with a professional writer, you will determine what makes you stand out from anyone else who serves the same customer base. How do you differentiate yourself?

Following is a basic outline for a branding story:

- First Paragraph: Explain your business.
- Second Paragraph: Explain why your business is different.

- Third Paragraph: Provide your personal business background and explain why your expertise is important to your business.

- Fourth Paragraph: Give a broad overview of your industry and how you excel.

- Fifth Paragraph: Wrap up your business's expertise and why your customers should appreciate it.

2. Your Target Audience

Many small business owners are so busy with their daily responsibilities they take little time to determine their exact target audience. To do this, ask yourself these questions:

- Are your customers other businesses or individuals?
- If they're individuals, how old are they?
- Are they equally split among men and women?
- How much education do they have?
- What is their net worth?
- What is their household income?
- How do they communicate with you? For example, do they prefer phone calls, snail mail, texts, emails or social media messaging?
- Why do they use your services?

Once you have a defined target audience, write a paragraph or two of that description. File it away with your business marketing information. You'll continually refer to this target audience, as you work with a content writer or another marketing professional to create a variety of written communications.

After you have written this information, you can decide which content marketing tips in this book will work best. For example, if most of your customers are over 65 years old, then social media may not be the best way to communicate with them. (Fewer people over 65 use social media than any other adult group.) You may want to consider direct mail for those customers. If most of your customers are younger than 30, then you'll need to be on Facebook, Twitter and many other social media sites that appeal to them.

3. YOUR ELEVATOR PITCH

Now that you've done the difficult work of writing your brand's story and examining your target audience, how can you succinctly verbalize a description of your business that emphasizes its unique differences?

Your elevator pitch is, simply, three or four sentences that you would use to describe your business if you were on an elevator traveling six floors with an important, new acquaintance.

Even though elevator pitches are almost always used during conversation, it helps any successful businessperson to put words on paper as you practice talking about yourself and your business.

Section II
Refresh Your Website

Once you have written your brand's story and defined your target audience, you'll be well focused to begin re-energizing your website. If you already have a website but haven't updated it in the last three years, it's time to refresh it. Is your current website still working for today's business world? Is it easy to read on mobile devices? Does it link in your Twitter feed? Does it allow for blog posts? Get started by creating a website map.

4. A Website Plan

Talk to your writer or a web project coordinator. Either of these people can help you organize your thoughts so that you can create a basic website map. Of course, a writer can also help you write the content that will be needed for a refreshed website and she or he may also help you locate the technical help that you need to accomplish the modern visual effect important in today's marketplace.

Generally, a website map will look like a flow chart that diagrams the basic information you want on the web. Here's an example of how it might look:

Home Page

About | Staff | Services | News | Blog | Contact

(Under each heading, make a note about the staff that will be featured, the products or services that you offer and any other pertinent information.)

As you're creating your plan, think about the visuals that you may want to include. Your home page is an important place, perhaps you'll want a dramatic design here, an oversized photo or a slide show. An independent graphic designer can help you with the design and freelance photographers can help with photos.

Spend some time looking at modern websites that you admire and take notes about why you like them. Remember, we now live in a highly visual society so anything that you post on your website should be of exemplary quality because it reflects the quality that your business brings.

Some business owners get overly concerned about creating a mobile app for their company. However, if you are using modern techniques, such as HTML-5 (also called a website with responsive design) then there's probably no reason to create an app. Websites done with HTML-5 coding will appear in a good format for mobile devices. Your web designer can help you understand today's digital market and whether you also need an app.

5. Slide Shows

Websites can easily be re-energized with great visuals that pull in your audience. Let's say you own a boat touring company. A large photo or a slide show featuring the scenery along your tour will help engage your target audience.

A good slide show takes project coordination and an independent writer may be capable of helping you pull together all of the pieces involved. First, you'll need professional quality photographs. Hire a professional photographer to get the best photos possible. Don't forget to add a caption of a sentence or two to each photo that will be shown on your website.

6

6. BIOGRAPHIES

In today's highly linked world, we want to know as much as possible regarding any business alliance. Therefore, posting brief biographies about your staff and your board of directors, if you have one, on your website will help form stronger bonds between your business and your customers.

A staff or director biography should be no more than 300 words talking about each person, his or her education, strengths and role in your business. Each staff member may add something fun about themselves, such as their hobbies or family information. Most people find it difficult to write about themselves, so you'll want to assign this duty to an outside writer.

Having biographies available for key staff members can also enhance your ability to promote your business in other ways. We'll discuss some of those opportunities with tips later in this book.

7. Resumes

In some industries it works well to post a full resume for yourself and other important members of your staff. For example, if you're a physician or an attorney who has published a lot of articles or participated in break-through research projects, then you'll want to communicate that information to customers and clients so that they understand your skills and expertise. This is what helps you differentiate yourself from your competition.

This is an excellent opportunity to take a close look at your latest resume and bring it up to date. With the help of a skilled writer, you can incorporate important information that may have evolved during the recent digital tsunami. For example, if you're a pediatrician with a large Twitter following, that's something worth talking about. Do you blog on LinkedIn? Then mention that on your resume.

When redesigning your business's website, you can put a link at the bottom of your bio that says "More Information" and add your resume to an additional web page linked there. You can do the same for any other staff member with significant experiences and expertise.

8. BLOGS

Everyone's a blogger. You may have heard this but it's not true. If you're a real estate agent and you're the only real estate agent in your community who's blogging to let your target audience know about the current real estate market and all that involves, then you're doing a good job of making yourself stand apart from your competition.

Generally, you'll want to address one small topic in 4-10 paragraphs, two or three times a week. As a real estate agent, for example, you might choose to talk about the fall of interest rates on Monday, the abundance of three-bedroom homes on the market on Wednesday, and a special weekend open house on Friday. Unless you are blogging on LinkedIn, remember to promote a link to your blog on social media.

9. FAQ SHEETS

Go back to your business's branding story. Are there questions about your business that still can be answered?

A FAQ sheet often gives quick answers to questions that your customers and clients may have about your business or matters related to your business. Your branding story and your target audience are only the starting points to any number of quick facts that you can provide to your customers.

If you're an investment broker, for example, you can use your FAQ sheet to give some insights regarding a new investment year. If you're a podiatrist, you can use FAQs to provide the signs and symptoms of a particular foot ailment. If you're an attorney, you can provide FAQs involving the legalities involved in any real estate transaction.

Whatever profession you represent, there are likely many opportunities to create FAQ sheets.

10. EVERGREEN STORIES

As the owner of a business, you should be well versed in a number of topics in which you can educate your target audience and portray yourself as an expert in the field. Evergreen stories are those that are pertinent to your business at any time of year, during any situation.

Part of the challenge of running a sustainable business in a competitive environment is standing out from the crowd. Developing a small library of evergreen stories that you post to your website, link to social media, use as background for media releases and other such projects, will help you do that.

For example, if you own a plant nursery, an evergreen story can discuss the cycle of plants and those that grow best in your region. If you have a tutoring business, you can project yourself as an expert when you discuss various learning disabilities and ways to help potential students who have them.

A dentist may have tips he or she can share with a target audience about good dental hygiene, especially if it's around Halloween when everyone is eating candy. A chef/

restaurateur can discuss any number of nutrition habits and a real estate agent can talk about topics such as staging a house for sale.

Once you decide which topics you'd like to address, talk to your writer about ways that you can present this information so that it's interesting and informative to your target audience. Of course, as each story is finished, post it to your website's news area.

As you re-energize your website, be sure you emphasize your business's unique attributes and the reasons that your customers and clients continue to return.

SECTION III
UPGRADE YOUR SOCIAL MEDIA

Look back at the last six months and review the successes and failures that your business has had on social media. Can you document which posts work well and which do not? Do you know how many fans "like" your business?

Social media posts, alone, are not difficult. But, you should have a mission and specific goals set if you're planning to integrate social media into your overall editorial schedule and marketing plan. Start with a social media audit and examine today's best opportunities for creating a strategic social media plan.

11

11. A Social Media Audit

To do a social media audit, assign a college intern, a freelance writer or someone else who is savvy to social (listed in numbers 13 to 19) to assess how many posts are made each week, if they are well written and if they seem to have a marketing goal.

If possible, look at the social media pages belonging to your key employees. Are they doing a good job at representing themselves in relationship to your business? For example, look at LinkedIn and see if someone identifies herself or himself as an employee of your company.

Good social media for a business depends on developing a strong following. The people who follow you because they like your brand are called brand evangelists. Employees are the first people who should be your brand evangelists. If they like their jobs then they should be willing to link themselves with your brand.

Do your employees have social media accounts? I was surprised during one recent social media audit to discover that the director of advertising at a local newspaper had only one link on LinkedIn.

Your social media audit may reveal that you need to convene a staff meeting to emphasize the importance of it in your business. The quick ascendance of social media in the last five years has left many people thinking that it's purely personal when, in fact, it can have a lot to do with building business.

12. A Strategic Social Media Plan

A professional writer with good social media skills may be the person best able to help you shape a strategic social media plan. This person can develop a calendar of social media posts, pinpoint which media will be used and what those posts should involve. Your social media plan can be done a month at a time or you may want to build your strategy for a three-month period. Incorporate give-aways, promotions, contests and other interactive fun that keep your fans and friends engaged.

Following are the most viable social media options for business. You may want to integrate many of them into your brand strategy. Keep in mind that all social media, of course, is global. So, the messages you post about your business will be viewed by people all over the world. Don't forget, too, that most social media sites offer strategic advertising possibilities.

13. FACEBOOK

The largest of all social media sites, Facebook, now has more than 699 million people who visit the site every day. Facebook has more women who are members than men, by about 10 percentage points. And, Facebook is still the top ranking social media for teens with 84 percent of people who are 18 to 29 years old using it. (Only 45 percent of people over 65 are on Facebook.)

Your business can have a Facebook page for free and it's important to keep that page updated and current because of the audience this media delivers. Due to Facebook's algorithms, paid advertising on this medium will help you reach more people than simply posting. Google "Facebook advertising" to locate information about this possibility.

14. LINKEDIN

Considered the top way to interact with other professionals, LinkedIn has more than 300 million members and more than 12 million small business professionals. The audience is largely between 30 and 49 years old. They are well-educated professionals who are working their way up the ladder. LinkedIn is also an opportunity to get others to write testimonials regarding their work with you.

Linking with others here can help you develop a strong bond with your target audience, especially if you're in a business that sells products or services to other businesses. In fact, LinkedIn is the most effective social media for connecting with other business owners. It also offers you the ability to blog and purchase advertising.

15. TWITTER

Twitter has 271 million monthly users and 78 percent of those who access Twitter do so via their mobile devices. Generally, more men than women use Twitter. This website proclaims itself a great tool for connecting businesses with their clients and the website even offers *The Small Business Guide to Twitter*.

Joining Twitter is also important because it can provide you quick access to information that could affect your business. It has archival possibilities. Do you feel tremors? Is there an earthquake? Search #earthquake and you may see a ripple effect of reports as the quake crosses the region. Is there a severe snow storm crossing the country? Search #snowstorm and see if there's any chatter.

Hashtags (also known as the pound sign) are important when using both Facebook and Twitter, as they allow you to categorize posts about your business or certain topics. For example, any post on these two social platforms should include your business's name after the hashtag, such as #RSRockMedia. If I were staging a book launch for this title, I might use the hashtag #50WaysLaunchParty.

16. INSTAGRAM

A highly visual media that focuses on photo sharing, rather than text, Instagram has over 300 million users. There's an important edge with this social media. One study found that 83 percent of teens from wealthy households were on Instagram. If that's the audience you're looking to capture, then consider posting photos to Instagram that are important to your marketing strategy.

17. PINTEREST

Another visually driven social media, Pinterest has been called a digital scrapbook for its 70-some million users, most of whom are women. Users pin their favorites on their pages and can share that page with others. It's a good way to do some viral marketing if you own a small boutique or have specific products to sell.

Pinterest is the latest social media to add advertising. Let's say you have just opened a business that sells olive oils. An artistic photograph featuring bottles of oil and a few recipes posted to Pinterest can get your business off to a more interesting start.

18. YOUTUBE

YouTube claims more than a billion viewers each month. One study found that for ages 18 to 34 years old, YouTube now reaches more people than any cable television station. Twenty-five percent of YouTube views come from mobile devices, too, making this another media that gets used on the go. Generally, YouTube has more female users.

For your own business, you can create a YouTube channel where you upload videos and then link them into your website.

19. VINE

A video-sharing app now owned by Twitter, Vine videos are generally short—about six seconds long. This is the only major social media site that is not yet selling ad spots.

20. SOCIAL MEDIA POSTS

Social media literacy is different from other kinds of writing. With limited character space, you'll want to work with a writer who knows how to put a lot of information in as few words as possible—with a flare that solicits likes and comments from other viewers.

Once you understand each social media, you can determine if it will become part of your Strategic Social Media Plan. Then, figure out how you'll release interesting and pertinent posts that elicit engagement from your fans and followers.

21. Social Media Engagement

A top priority for your social media plan should be engagement. Following is a quick guide for being sure that your company is engaged with your audience on any of the social media that you plan to use. If you're looking for an easy way to cover your social media bases, hire interns to write your posts and then give them the following plan.

On Facebook:

- "Like" Facebook posts made by friends and followers.
- "Share" posts, photos and videos created by other reputable media regarding the news and odd stories of the day.
- "Friend" reputable local media.
- "Comment" on others' posts.
- Post Happy Birthday messages to fans when appropriate.

On LinkedIn:

- Create a business LinkedIn Fan page.
- Build an archive of visuals that link to your website.
- Congratulate people who are links when they've made career changes.
- Post daily comments that are news links from reputable publications.
- Consider blogging on LinkedIn.

On Twitter:

- Tweet news links from local media and your industry.
- Tweet congratulatory messages when appropriate.
- Reply and retweet other messages that reflect on your business or industry.

On Pinterest:

- Update your Pinterest page with industry related visuals.
- Pin items of interest to your customers and clients.
- Build your following by incorporating links to Facebook and Twitter pages

On Instagram:

- Update your account with photos.
- Post images of your business's special events and occasions.
- Build your Instagram following by integrating messages with your Facebook and Twitter posts.

- Pay attention to what your friends post. Engage in conversation, when it makes sense.

On Vine or YouTube:

- Engage with others who have related businesses by viewing and sharing their videos, when appropriate.

- Create mobile videos that can be quickly posted to Facebook and Twitter. Add these to your YouTube channel.

- Promote your videos on your website and in your other social media.

- Vine videos are easily posted to Twitter. When you post such a video, be sure to include a hashtag that will guide people back to your website.

22. SOCIAL MEDIA ANALYTICS

Each social media site offers ways to find your analytics. A quick Google search of a term such as "Facebook analytics" will help you find Facebook Insights. Social media analytics for the sites that you use will help you determine who's watching you and if you're reaching your target audience. In some cases, such as LinkedIn, you'll be required to become a paid user to get the most specific information about your viewers.

For any business owner, it's important to keep careful watch on your social media data. Today, entire companies are being built around the use of digital analytics, which are also known as metrics or quantitative analytics. The bottom line? The person who is overseeing your social media strategy should be able to help you analyze your data to make improvements in your social media communications.

Section IV
Mine for Golden Opportunities

To appear to be on the cutting edge of your industry, it's important that you keep up on the latest research in your field. As a small business owner, though, you may find that your time is sparse to do so. Consider hiring a researcher or writer to gather information that will provide you with reasons to connect with your target audience, talk to local news media and become known as an expert with an outstanding knowledge in your field.

23. RESEARCH REPORTS

Start by having your researcher explore a particular topic of current interest and submit a summary to you. For example, if you're a pediatrician, ask your writer to research the recent resurgence of tuberculosis among children. Your researcher should be able to find the facts and figures for any health ailment by checking out governmental websites such as the Centers for Disease Control and the National Institutes of Health to gather the information that is needed.

Then, ask your writer to interview you so that you can provide a few quotes regarding the signs and symptoms of the disease, the possible cures and other relevant information. The length of a research report may vary from 500-2,500 words. Of course, you'll want to post the report on your website and link it to your social media.

The information in this report can also be used as the basis for media releases and other content marketing materials such as white papers, case studies and even e-books.

24. CASE STUDIES

A case study will range from 500-750 words with a focus on one particular customer or client and the success that he or she had using your product or service.

Let's say that you own an organic farm. A local chef purchases all of his produce from your farm and he notices that, not only is it a healthier option, but the shelf life for your produce is far longer than the shelf life for produce purchased in grocery stores.

Having a case study written about this chef and his success with your produce will help inform other local chefs about your services. In addition, a professional writer can find other facts and figures that support this chef's story about the health benefits of using local, organic produce.

Case studies should be added to the news section of your website, promoted on your social media and used as background for media releases, which we'll discuss later. They can help you communicate your expertise on a variety of subjects.

25. WHITE PAPERS

Formerly a term used mainly in academic circles, white papers have become another way to establish your dominance in the world of content marketing. They provide an opportunity to succinctly write about the details uncovered in your research report or new research that has recently been announced.

White papers provide more of an overview of your expertise, rather than a singular viewpoint expressed in a case study. Generally, white papers are used to persuade your audience to purchase a product or service. They can range from 500 words to 2,500.

For example, a vintner may write a white paper exuding the positive health benefits of drinking red wine. A marketing professional might write a white paper about the importance of a new social media. White papers help you become an authority in your field by discussing the facts and other information that will draw customers to your business.

Section V
Get Visuals and Sound

Opportunities abound in our highly digitized and mobile world to share your expertise and knowledge with people around the globe. How many times have you been standing in line for coffee, pulled out your mobile phone and scrolled Facebook looking for nuggets of interest? Use social media to lure your target audience into learning more about your business by sharing links to your visual presentations.

26. Power Point Slide Shows

Speaking engagements and public presentations are good ways to make your brand stand out. A professional writer can help you focus on the main points in a presentation, translating those to an appealing slide presentation that will be attractive to your audience. (For those who are shy about speaking in public, an attractive Power Point presentation will also mean that most in the audience will be watching the slide show instead of you.)

 All of the information that has been gathered for research reports, white papers, case studies and other materials can provide a strong basis for your Power Point show.

But a word of caution: Too many presenters load down their Power Point presentations with too much verbiage and statistics. Each Power Point slide should be focused on one to three key points that keep your presentation on track. Then, you can add anecdotes as you speak.

Once your speaking engagement is over, load your Power Point presentation onto Slideshare.com, link it to your website and promote it on social media.

27. VIDEOS

Videos are powerful vehicles in today's marketing world. If they are entertaining, they can spread virally via social media once you upload them to YouTube and splash them across your Facebook, Twitter and other social accounts. Videos can be used to demonstrate a product or service, give a tour of your facility, educate potential clients on special topics and other things.

First, though, create a plan for the story that you'll present. Once you decide the topic you'd like to address, your content writer can help you write an outline and perhaps an entire script, if needed.

Online videos should not be longer than three minutes. Generally, a video script will incorporate about four lines of text (about 75 characters per line) for each 15 seconds. So, if you're producing a minute-long script, you'll want about 16 lines of text. For a three-minute script, you'll want about 48 lines of text. As you can see, writing a video script will require writing a succinct message— good videos don't accommodate wordiness.

By working on a script with your writer, you can incorporate your overall branding story as well as some background about yourself and the product or service that you want to feature.

During this process, your writer should be able to help you locate a videographer who will do the filming. Or, if your writer has the programming required to edit videos, a decent video shoot may be done with any mobile device. Either way, the person who will do the filming and the editing should understand the script and the visuals that will be needed to accompany the text.

A children's summer camp director may want to provide a video showing an excerpt from a camp day. Or, a vintner may want to show how wine is produced.

A real estate agent may want to create well-done video tours of houses that are up for sale. A dentist may even want to show a cavity being filled.

Perhaps you own a local pizza shop and you want to do a humorous video with your chef and a few customers. Share that video on social media with your customers and they may share it with others. Soon, everyone who sees it may have a craving for pizza.

28. WEBCASTS

Webcasts are informational sessions that are presented to potential customers and clients. They are often used for trainings on specific projects or topics. For example, a marketing expert may provide a webcast about effectively using social media.

An entrepreneurial podiatrist I know has done a series of short webcasts talking about various foot ailments and potential solutions for them. (You can then purchase some of these solutions from his website.)

Again, a writer can help you create a detailed outline for the project. Decide if you or someone else will moderate the topic. Perhaps you'd like for someone to interview you during a webcast, or maybe you want to interview other guests.

Once the format of your webcast is decided, outline the main points to be discussed, decide if you'll integrate screen shots or other graphics, and if you'll incorporate Power Point slides during the presentation. Depending on your topic, you may want a complete script written.

Webcasts can range in time, from three minutes to a half hour. There are numerous companies, such as gotomeeting. com, that will allow you to set up a webcast and record it for archival use. If you've created a longer webcast, you may want to take the time to edit it into smaller sections that can be archived or linked on your website. There is a variety of editing software available on the market and a digital expert, such as your web guru, should be able to help you.

29. PODCASTS

Podcasts are audio recordings that can be aired live or archived for later use. A podcast may involve music or voice. Think of a podcast as an opportunity to talk with an employee about an upcoming trend in your business while he or she is driving to work.

To create a succinct message, again, you may need to create a good script that you've practiced before actually recording the message. The time involved in a good podcast is similar to those involved in video and webcasts. For every four typed lines, you've used 15 seconds of talk time.

A podcast, too, can vary in time ranging from only a few minutes to those as long as a half hour. A technology expert or your web guru should be able to help you with the equipment you need to produce top quality podcasts that can be downloaded via iTunes and other methods. Of course, you'll want to also archive or link any podcasts on your website.

Section VI
Connect With Community Media

Newspapers and magazines, as well as television and radio stations in your community, are all over social media day and night. Don't ignore the local and national media as you're rethinking your brand's story.

Mainstream news organizations have spent millions of dollars figuring out how to keep readers engaged. There was a time in recent years that it seemed that community newspapers and local television stations would disappear. Instead they are all busy morphing into highly digitized community news organizations—with an engaged following that includes thousands of people every day. Consider which media will help you reach your target audience.

It's not difficult to engage with local media via Tweets and Facebook messages. Use the following tips, though, to go a little deeper with your relationships. Media reporters tend to connect with people they know.

30. LETTERS OF INTRODUCTION

Do you think you're a unique expert who should be known to the local media? Work with your writer to develop a Letter of Introduction to local newspaper and magazine editors, as well as radio and television producers so that they know your areas of expertise. First, make sure that they know you're a reader (or a viewer) who admires their publication (or show).

Within the email, list six or eight good story topics that you can address in an upcoming issue or program. If you're approaching your local television or radio station, be sure to give links to a YouTube video that demonstrates your presentation skills.

31. Media Releases

Media releases to local newspaper editors, magazine editors, and television and radio producers are the best way to keep traditional media apprised of your business—and this will help grow your business's brand. If your company is featured on local media, you'll quickly be thrust into a limelight that includes thousands of viewers and readers.

The features you've produced about evergreen topics can be coupled with elements of your branding story to create timely and pertinent media releases of interest to your local newspapers, magazines, television and radio, and other media outlets.

A professional writer—including any former journalist who has read many media releases during his or her career—is an expert at creating releases that grab the attention of your local editors and producers at radio and television stations.

Every media release should have a news hook. For example, if you own a landscaping company and you've recently become aware of an invasive insect that will harm all apple trees in your region, send a media release out on this topic and you can quickly become the expert who will address this issue for your local editors and producers.

The business owner who presents such topics to the media in the most timely manner is usually the person who gets the most media attention—whether that's a feature in the local newspaper's business section or a spot on a local news program. Any amount of media attention will help your business build a strong brand with its target audience.

In addition to being timely, the first two paragraphs of a well-written media release should address the five Ws:

- Who is involved?
- What is the issue?
- When has it become an issue?
- Where is it occurring?
- Why is it happening?

Don't forget to include some background information about your business. You can easily do that by taking information already written in your branding story. Generally, a media release will probably be 500-700 words.

Once you are happy with the media release that is written, ask your writer to email it to the local editors and producers who may benefit from it. Community newspapers and television stations like to have local experts that they can quote at various times.

Of course, you'll also want to post the media release in the news section of your website. Additionally, a link to any article about you or your business that runs in the local media also should be noted in the news section of your website and on your social media.

32. MEDIA ADVISORIES

Media advisories are shorter than press releases and they're generally distributed to alert the media that a special event is about to occur. For example, alert the media that you're appearing as the keynote speaker at the local community foundation's annual gala. It may announce that your company will have an open house at your new office. A media advisory can help you stay in touch with anyone that is covering the news and events of your community.

At this point, you already have a significant amount of information on your website that may interest the local media. Is there an upcoming holiday that you can address? Consider creating a media advisory that is based on one of your evergreen topics. For example, a landscaper may issue an advisory about a chronic plant disease in your geographic location.

33. 12 Tips

Aside from evergreen topics, another way to approach a media release is to create a *12 Tips* list. For example, if you're a chef, you may want to write a column offering a local editor *12 Tips to Preserving Vegetables*.

If you're a veterinarian, you could suggest: *12 Tips to Treating Cats With Allergies*. The possibilities are endless. Your 12 Tips approach, of course, can be reduced to any number of tips that you can offer. By providing an occasional media story based on this 12-tip philosophy, you'll soon be known among your local media as the go-to source for interesting tips to use on a slow news day.

34. HOLIDAY FEATURES

Traditional media outlets are always looking for good holiday stories. Your media releases can be designed around any specific holiday. A bakery might publicize: *Easy Cookies for the December Holiday Season.* Or, a pediatrician may release an advisory such as: *How to Prevent July Fourth Fireworks Accidents.*

35. Letters to the Editor

There is no more gracious way to interact with your local media than to write a Letter to the Editor thanking them, or the community, for a special act of kindness. For example, if a local reporter does a feature about your business, respond with a Letter to the Editor offering praise for the reporter and the entire newspaper staff.

If you're a business owner, write a Letter to the Editor pointing out a significant act by one of your town council members. You may find it easy to brainstorm with your writer about this easy way to reach the significant number of readers of your local community newspaper.

Letters to the Editor should be three to five paragraphs long. Be sure you get to the point in the first paragraph, back up your rationale in the second paragraph, and then give a little of your personal or business background before you close.

36. Op-Ed Columns

Sometimes there's an opportunity to publish a column in your local newspaper that responds to a local or national event. This is another way to reach thousands of readers every day. (Of course, you'll always want to link any magazine or newspaper articles to your social media posts, too.)

For example, if you own a company that's developing clean energy or you're an attorney who represents environmental interests, then you might want to write an op-ed column that opposes the environmentally questionable drilling method called hydraulic fracturing (also known as fracking). If you own a gas or oil business, you may want to take the opposite stance, demonstrating the awesome modern innovation involved in fracking.

SECTION VII
ENGAGE WITH AN
EDITORIAL CALENDAR

Developing an editorial calendar that integrates your social media plan with blog posts, media releases, e-books and other information is imperative. With the writer you hire, you will want to sketch an editorial plan on a calendar. Will you write blog entries three times a week? Will you plan events that need promoted? Will you use social media to promote your blog and your events? If so, which social media will you use?

37. E-NEWSLETTERS

Within your editorial calendar, you may want to schedule intermittent e-newsletters. Templates can be found at ConstantContact.com and similar websites. These programs also can help you connect with your email database. With a quick integration of your logo, the newsletter can begin looking as though it's part of your brand.

Stories in your e-newsletter can include a mix of recent news in your industry, short bios of valuable employees and stories about your company. Some stories may only involve introductory paragraphs and links to your website or additional news sources. Don't forget to add a calendar segment mentioning upcoming sales and special events.

Always keep in mind as you're working with a writer to create a professional e-newsletter or a printed newsletter: The ultimate goal is to connect with customers and clients who can help you build your business.

38. E-MAIL BLASTS

When you have one, brief bit of information—such as a synopsis of a research report or a recently won award—consider blasting it out to your email database. Retailers such as J.Crew, Gap and others often use e-mail blasts to promote specific sales. Your loyal customers and clients may be pleased to be in-the-know about important news that you blast to them.

39. NICHE MAGAZINES

With today's digital information proliferation, how can you stand out from the crowd? Your business can produce its own print magazine.

A few real estate agents I know sell expensive homes and produce print magazines of 32 to 112 pages, at least once a year.

Why print? Because these real estate agents recognize that, with the help of professional writers, photographers and designers, they can show their homes in a beautifully printed magazine that those receiving will be reluctant to throw away. As you may know, high-resolution photographs have fewer pixels than those on the web, so viewers generally can see a better picture if it's in print.

Producing your own magazine can be an expensive endeavor, but talk with your local or regional magazine publisher—or a printer—who can help determine if a magazine is a worthwhile investment. Many regional and city magazine publishers can even help you distribute to upscale households in a targeted area so that your mailing costs can be minimized while your audience is maximized.

Producing your own magazine can be a costly adventure, ranging to $10,000 and more. If producing an entire magazine just isn't in your budget consider a magazine insert that will accomplish many of your goals with a more affordable pricetag.

The release of a special print product should be followed with social media chatter. A photograph of the magazine's cover posted to Facebook may trigger online engagement from your dedicated customers and clients.

40. NEWSPAPER INSERTS

Community newspapers still go to anywhere from 3,000 to more than 200,000 households each day. That's a big audience that can be reading about your brand.

Consider producing a newspaper insert or a supplement that gets delivered with your community newspaper. Advertisements can be any size on a page, of course, but supplements can range from four pages to many more and can be easily delivered in targeted zip codes, perhaps keeping expenses even lower.

A good writer who has worked as a journalist can help you understand the deadlines involved in publishing print, the stories you'll need to have written for a special supplement or niche publication, and the hi-resolution photographs that will be needed to make this a successful and worthwhile publication.

41. ANNUAL REPORTS

Public companies and nonprofit businesses must create annual reports that detail their finances. Thus, even small businesses should consider the annual report as a good opportunity to present your brand.

Is a newspaper supplement an option? Should you partner with a local magazine to produce an informational piece that you can continue distributing throughout the year? Will a 12-page brochure fulfill this need?

Whatever method you desire, use the annual report as another opportunity to present your brand's story in an authentic and riveting manner. Include good storytelling about the deeds that you've done, engage the customers you serve and give fascinating facts in an easily digestible manner about those who benefit from your business or nonprofit.

42. BROCHURES

Yes, there's still a reason to produce good brochures: People read print. Literacy studies have shown that they read print, in fact, easier than they read on a digital screen with a higher rate of comprehension. Our digital overload has us paying closer attention when something is now in print. Most importantly, in today's world a brochure helps you tell your story with a good design that is complemented with hi-resolution photos.

When are brochures most helpful? If you're a political candidate and you want to directly mail voters, use a well-designed brochure that tells your personal story. If you're promoting your business in a room of potential clients or you're an invited speaker to a special event, a brochure can succinctly explain your business or cause.

Today's printing capabilities provide many opportunities to make a unique and impressionable print brochure at a reasonable cost. Because so few businesses are producing nice brochures, this nearly forgotten medium provides a grand way to stand out from the crowd.

43. ADVERTISEMENTS

Unique and interesting advertisements for social media, newspapers, magazines, television, radio and even billboards can be developed with good design and engaging copy to tell your brand's story in a consistent manner across all platforms. Even though advertisements have been around for a long time, today's information proliferation makes good design and consistent brand imaging more important than ever before.

44. E-Books

To gain an even broader platform for your brand, hire someone to ghostwrite an e-book. Let's say that you are a real estate agent. E-books can be short, so you could write a 5,000-word e-book about staging your home for sale. Or, a plumber could write an e-book that gives plumbing advice to people who are in critical situations. Why do kitchen sinks always clog on holidays just before guests arrive?

After your book has been written and well edited, use Bibliocrunch.com, Smashwords.com, Ingramspark.com or another e-book platform to upload your e-book to Amazon and other places. Who knows? You could sell enough e-books that would warrant eventually self-publishing your book in print.

45. Printed Books

There are many reasons why you may want to produce a book in print, not the least being that it will look great on your bookshelf. But today's publishing environment makes it a challenge for many experts to get book contracts the old-school way, complete with an advance and royalty checks that roll in on a regular basis.

Thankfully, there are a lot of print-on-demand publishers that will publish a small quantity of books at a reasonable cost to you so that you can sell them on your website, during book fairs, at community bookstores, during speaking engagements and book signings. You can also sell your self-published printed books on Amazon and other sites, too. If you're working with a well-published writer, he or she can guide you through the book publishing process.

When your book or e-book is finally finished, consider its launch a reason for celebration. You may want to plan a launch party, give away bookmarks, announce your book's availability on social media, alert local traditional media and post a cover of your book on your website and a link to order it.

Section VIII
Power Up Your Marketing Plan

If your head is spinning with all the possibilities of promoting your brand, that's not unusual. In today's digital environment there are amazing opportunities to tell your business's story so that it stands out. But planning and good organization are key.

Everything that's been discussed so far in this book, of course, is part of your marketing plan. In this section, we'll look at how you pull together your social media strategy, an editorial calendar and other parts of your marketing campaign.

46. A Marketing Plan

Use an Excel sheet to begin integrating all the aspects of your marketing plan. This sheet should include all areas of marketing, including events, speaking engagements and other opportunities that allow you promote your business's plan. Don't forget to also include all parts of your editorial calendar, which will range from your blog entries to your social media posts to your media releases.

47. Speaking Engagements

Whether you're scheduled as a keynote speaker, a panelist or a workshop presenter, these are opportunities for you to talk about your brand.

Be well prepared, because in today's world, you will speak to a group of people who will likely be tweeting, posting your photo on Instagram, or putting out videos on Facebook. (You may even want to take along someone who can tweet or message about your appearance on your own social media.) Be sure that you're focused on the key points in your message so that any wide distribution of your comments reflects well on your business's brand.

A writer can not only help you write such a speech, or prepare for a workshop, but he or she may also be willing to research and make contacts for you at various organizations in the community that may be looking for keynote speakers. Whether it's the local Chamber of Commerce, Rotary, Kiwanis or another community service organization, many are in need of regular speakers.

48. EVENTS

As social media has become more important, face-to-face connections have become more valuable. Studies have shown that face-to-face meetings allow you to connect with your target audience and build trust, important components to making sales. Face-to-face meetings help build relationships.

Schedule some fun, interactive opportunities to show your clients and customers that you like to see them. Open houses, special sales, give-aways, community health fairs, book fairs and other festivals and festivities provide great opportunities to showcase your business brand.

Hire a project manager or an event planner to seek out events or plan your own special events that target your specific audience. These events provide a reason for you to create social media chatter and engage with your customers and clients on a virtual level, too.

Don't forget, of course, that the local media should be alerted. You can do that with a media release, a media advisory or by including specific invitations to your media contact list. Finally, be sure that your event has live social media coverage so that you can continue to connect with those who are not attending.

49. SPONSORSHIPS

Nonprofit organizations and some businesses are continually looking for partners to help sponsor upcoming events. This is an excellent way to get your brand in front of people and garner some goodwill in the process. Carefully selecting a sponsorship opportunity will help you form strategic alliances with others in your community and will add to your brand's authentic story.

Consider sponsoring a Little League team, a philanthropic gala or a golf outing—all depending, of course, on the best fit for your desired target audience. All sponsorships provide opportunities to put your name in front of a lot of people but be sure you read any agreement carefully to determine how much visibility your brand will be given.

50. PROMOTIONAL ITEMS

Branded notebooks, pens, coffee cups, flash drives, candy bars and other useful items are good ways to get your brand noticed in unique ways. Have you missed this opportunity for brand exposure? If so, companies available that offer branded items can easily be found with a quick Google search.

One of my favorite campaigns involved miniature footballs that had the logo for a local medical center printed on them. High school cheerleaders threw these balls to the crowds during football games. It was an easy campaign that had staying power as we envisioned these footballs lying around the homes and yards in this community for many years to come.

Certainly, a marketing event such as the one mentioned above provides plenty of opportunity to tell your brand's story. Use social media and connect with your community media to see the ripple effects that can result from a unique and creative event like this one that is focused on an inexpensive promotional opportunity.

About the Author

Sherry Beck Paprocki is an award-winning journalist, author, social media strategist, content provider and small business entrepreneur. As the vice president of the American Society of Journalists and Authors she has become aware of a confluence in today's writing marketplace: businesses and nonprofits have a significant need for good content and plenty of former journalists and other entrepreneurial writers are looking for work.

She developed *Content Marketing: 50 Ways to Tell Your Story*, in part, so that big and small brands can find the best, most experienced storytellers available to create their content.

As the president and founder of R.S. Rock Media, Inc., Paprocki develops strategic brand messaging for digital and print products produced by mainstream media, small businesses, big personalities and nonprofit organizations. She has served as a writer and editor for several publications, as well as an interim publisher for *San Antonio Magazine* and the *Granville Sentinel* newspaper in Ohio.

As a co-author of *The Complete Idiot's Guide to Branding Yourself* (Alpha, 2009), Paprocki and her husband, magazine publisher Ray Paprocki, explored the emerging world of strategic personal branding with the advent of social media. Since the book's publication, Sherry Beck Paprocki has immersed herself into social media research and how it plays into strategic storytelling. She serves as a senior lecturer on the topic for Otterbein University.

A frequently requested speaker regarding the social media tsunami and strategic branding, she has addressed writers around the country, physicians and other medical personnel, school superintendents and principals, public relations professionals, the women's leadership conference of the Ohio Bar Association, career counselors, regional media staffs, interior designers and student entrepreneurs.

Paprocki's teaching style encourages 360-learning, with audience members actively participating. In particular, she expresses appreciation to writers who helped develop this list of 50 things you need written during ASJA's Content Connections Conferences in Chicago in November 2014.

As a journalist and editor, Paprocki has won top honors from the Cleveland Press Association, the Ohio Society of Professional Journalists, the City and Regional Magazine Association (CRMA) and the Council for Advancement and Support of Education (CASE).

Her book about a big personal brand, *Oprah Winfrey: Talk Show Host and Media Magnate* (Chelsea House, 2006), was listed on the Voice of Youth Advocates Nonfiction Honor List. Also for Chelsea House, she has written books about other big name brands including Katie Couric, Bob Marley, Ellen DeGeneres, Michelle Kwan, Martha Stewart and more.